Marijuana Law in 4:20

by
Michael John Westerman

Cover & Contents © 2018 Michael John Westerman

Chapter I:
Key Dates & Data

Introductory Statement

The cannabis industry possesses the fuel needed by the American economy to rocket atop a cloud of smoke into a new era of unprecedented prosperity. The industrialization of marijuana across our great nation could revive the middle class in this post-Great Recession period and breath life back into the American Dream (home ownership with just one full-time job) through the national expansion of marijuana cultivation, production, commercialization, and distribution. The following words will give you all the key points you need to know about cannabis law in the U.S. of A. in a quick 4-chapter/20-page format one could with haste move through in all of about 4 minutes and 20 seconds, bespoke to the ADHD generation. I believe in the full legalization of marijuana to the point of national industrialization. I support the national sale of marijuana, and I recognize the intensely benevolent potential behind the taxation of marijuana to bankroll societally beneficial programs, namely education, plus food- and employment-assistance programs. No American should go hungry, unemployed, or under-educated, and the endless billions in potential represented by the marijuana industry can provide for these needs and many more across the United States.

Over the past two decades, I've witnessed the various entrepreneurial initiatives of the many impresarios and characters of the marijuana industry that I've come into contact with, having something of an affinity for the counter-culture myself. I was in California pursuing a since fizzled screenwriting career during the initial wave of legalization in terms of medical marijuana in the mid-00s, when a testament of "occasional headaches" or "hunger" and a $75 fee provided one a medical marijuana card and access to legit designer strains. Following that California dreamin' I shifted upwards from the Golden Coast into the Pacific Northwest, from a Japanese something or other into my first e34 5-series stick-shift BMW, the model but not build-out I still rock today. There I checked the medical legalization of Oregon in the hipster-haven of Portland, encountering the NCIA, the National Cannabis Industry Association and NORML, the National Organization for the Reform of Marijuana Laws. I applied to write propaganda for them, but they'd already sufficient mouths and fingers putting out words for them.

Returning to Massachusetts for a brief period in the early 10's I came to find friends legally growing medical marijuana in my home-state. Shifting down to Austin, Texas to escape winters for a handful of years, I observed the liberal pro-pot behavior of a rainbow city situated in a Red State with anti-marijuana laws strongly in place, and with an active NORML chapter. Moving northward with my two Texas cattle dogs, specifically Navy the cattle dog and Maureen the Chihuahua/Dachshund cattle dog, I stopped in Washington D.C. and experienced firsthand the token-based recreational marijuana model in place to satisfy the curiously organized regional policy concerning that whacky tobacky. One pays for the sticker with the delivery service's branding on it, not the satchel of cannabis products they give you afterwards; as if it could be any other way. Shifting into Massachusetts once more to attend law school and as the plan goes emerge a preeminent cannabis attorney, my eyes have reflected the legalization of recreational marijuana in the Commonwealth, and the roll-out of a shadow distribution system reminiscent of Washington D.C., awaiting the opening of dispensaries and the exercise of the true character of Taxachusetts, that of optimizing state-income through a relatively aggressive tax praxis.

Following is my compendium of marijuana law, policy, statute, a taste of my legal scholarly writing, and an original interview I conducted with the Tribal Leader of a federally-recognized American Indian Sovereign Nation, exploring the implications of legalization on the Reservations of the Native Tribes of North America in terms of the Tribal-State-Federal trinity of law, searching out the overlapping center of the Venn diagram in which industrialization satisfies the imperatives of all three. The data herein is current as of June 2018, although locate somewhere else for citing data as this is by no means meant to serve as an academic reference, and in the coming months I may publish "Cannabis Law Case Book: Clearing the Smoke" in which I'll present an up-to-date timeline of all the key cases relevant to cannabis law. Arriba.

KEY DATA

Following is a brief presentation of the essential data points one should know in terms of marijuana, including the modern lingo, street versus dispensary prices, usage rates, a timeline of the key dates through the evolution from illegal to recreational, and other key facts, providing us a frame through which to view the forthcoming statutes and cases, and my consideration of the fascinating and arcane sphere of Native American sovereignty and marijuana capitalism.

The Low Down

Marijuana is rather popular, in fact, quite a few people you know are doing it. THC makes you high, CBD alleviates pain. Weed can be sativa, a head high, indica, a body high, or a hybrid of the two. Potency varies from 10% low-quality plant to 90+% concentrates. It can be smoked, vaporized, or baked into "edibles". Actual weed is now called "flower", of which 3.5 grams is an eighth, 1/8 of an ounce, whereas 7 grams is a "quarter", 14 grams a "half", and upwards. Concentrates sell as "oil", "shatter", or "crumple", for $40-60/gram, and also as pre-fabricated cartridges, often medically- or CO/CA recreationally-sourced, 500mg for $50, with 250mg of that being pure THC, in general. Smoking cartridges is totally future, and also way hipster. The battery packs recharge via USB-drive. Greener technology indeed. Street prices for "flower", traditional marijuana nuggets and shake, are $30/eighth, $50/quarter, $90/half, $160/ounce, $5-600/quarter pound, $2,000-2,800 per pound. We're talking name-brand "Green Crack", "Sour Diesel", "Blue Dream", "Durban Poison", "Girl Scout Cookies"...

Since the advent of legalization street prices have dropped substantially. For example, in Boston in the early 00's, marijuana of equitable quality to the "flower" of today was selling for $70/eighth, $120/quarter, $200/half, $350/ounce, and $1,200 at minimum for a quarter pound, with pounds starting off at $3,000 but generally around $4,000 for top-quality as we have today. Prices in California at the time were only slightly lower, with street eighths going for $50-60, and dispensary-sourced eighths going for $60-85 straight-up, meaning no drop in price for volume increases. In legal states, street prices and dispensary prices have fallen lower, although tax-rates must be balanced so as to not make the ever present tax-free gray-market more appealing to the prospective consumer.

Prevalence of Use

The smoking of marijuana may take many forms, as with alcohol. Flower equals beer, concentrates equal shots. For some, occasionally partaking is more than sufficient to achieve the requisite effect. For others, whether medical or recreational, ongoing use is the norm. An occasional smoker may burn after work each day, or await the weekend for a day of Netflix, chilling, and choice munchies. Habitual smokers begin the day with a "wake and bake", and "maintain" throughout the day by "smoking up" regularly, each few hours at best. However the habit is manifested, quite a few Americans are about marijuana. In fact, an estimated 30 million Americans use marijuana, while some 20 million burn at minimum once monthly. 40% of all Americans have tried marijuana, and 5 million use it just about daily Madams and Sirs

Highest states: Alaska, Colorado, Oregon, and Vermont
Lowest states: Alabama, Kansas, and Louisiana

The Money

Marijuana has demonstrated vast economic potential for those States in which it has been legalized, and upon federal recognition of its true earnings potential, for the nation at large. In terms of taxes, Colorado levies 2.9% on medical, and around 30% for recreational. Washington State is at 44% on recreational weed. Crazy.

The revenue potential is also monstrous. In 2015 Colorado made some $120 million in taxes and fees from recreational marijuana on almost

$1 billion in sales, estimated to have had a positive $2.4 billion impact on the state. My vision of a thriving-wage middle-class is real, as 18,000 jobs have been created in Colorado alone due to marijuana. From July 2014 through June 2015 Washington State made $75 million in taxes and fees through recreational marijuana.

The earnings potential of marijuana must also be balanced against the cost of enforcement. Through legalization, enforcement becomes moot, and thus the related expenditures would fade and drift back into state budgets in worthier programs. The ACLU estimated that the 2010 costs alone for marijuana enforcement equaled some $3.6 billion. Lesson: legalize it.

The Prison and Incarceration Issue – I'll not be going there, but note, it's negative.

KEY DATES IN CANNABIS HISTORY
Medical Marijuana in Post-Bellum America

1870 – Marijuana included in the United States' Pharmacopoeia (nation's compendium of medical drugs), establishing the initial recognition of its medical value and application

1870-1890 – "Poison Laws" – patent medicine ingredient lists required, nothing outlawed, marijuana lumped into "narcotics" with cocaine and opiates, although not always singled out

1906 – Pure Food and Drug Act – marijuana included, labels must state presence/volume, dosage and purity standards offered up based on the Pharmacopoeia

Initial Period of Criminalization

1914 – Harrison Narcotics Tax Act – producers/importers of cocaine and opiates had to pay a tax, violation was up to 5 years in jail. Non-licensed possession, or non-medical sale, were made illegal, laying the foundation for the criminality of "narcotics", weed tacitly included

1932 – The Uniform Narcotic Drug Act – put control largely in the hands of States to enforce narcotics laws, as per the Federal Bureau of Narcotics, led by Commissioner Harry. J. Ansliger, who called "marihuana" a "national menace" and sought it be classified a narcotic, with states ultimately getting to choose once it was included on the list, with 2/3 of states doing so

1937 – Marihuana Tax Act – same effect as Harrison Tax Act, criminalizing non-medical/non-licensed sale/possession, 5 years in jail and up to $2,000 fine

The "War on Drugs"

1951 – Boggs Act – minimum sentencing – 2yrs for possession 1st offense – 5 years for 2nd offense – 10 years each additional offense. Jesus tap-dancing on water Christ

1956 – Narcotics Control Act – 5yr minimum sentence for marijuana known to have been brought into the U.S. illegally, and probation, parole, and suspension options eliminated for importation offenses, and… automatic presumption of illegal importation and knowledge

1961 – Singe Convention Treaty on Narcotic Drugs – International treaty globalizing the war on drugs and binding the United States against opiates, cocaine, and marijuana

1965 – non-medical marijuana illegal in all states

1969 – Marihuana Tax Act struck down as unconstitutional

1970 – Controlled Substance Act passed, marijuana made schedule I drug, relied upon the Commerce Clause

1973 – The Drug Enforcement Agency (DEA) Established

1984 – Comprehensive Crime Control Act – aggressive arrests, voluminous incarceration

1986 – Anti-Drug Abuse Act – the era of mandatory minimums – 100+ kgs of weed was 5 years and a fine up to $2 million, then 1,000+ kgs minimum of 10 years and $4 million. "Three Strikes" for marijuana. 1st possession short sentence and small fine. 2nd possession no less than 15 days to 2 years, and subsequent possession a 90 day minimum, potentially life for the third strike. They're out! Or in a cage rather with one hour out a day, with luck

Decriminalization

1972 – March – Michigan releases activist John Sinclair, aka "10 for 2", years for joints, given to an undercover female officer honeypot who'd arrested him after being his funky lady for weeks "enjoying" the counterculture life playing at "pretend", and entrapment. Narcs. The Michigan Supreme Court ruled that the conviction violated the Equal Protection Clauses of the United States and Michigan Constitutions, issuing an order for his release. The Court's rationale was that marijuana should not be treated in parallel to those pesky narcotics, heroin and cocaine

1972 – Marihuana Commission Report Issued – recommended elimination of criminal penalties for possession, supported by the American Bar Association. Nixon had appointed 9/13 of the members, yet of course was not down with the herb and violently opposed the counter-culture that he was too square and un-hip to ever get invited to any gatherings to enjoy, so naturally, the hater shall hate, but the ideological tide had elevated and begun to shift

1972 – Ann Arbor, Michigan – possession of marijuana a civil infraction, $5 fine

<u>1973</u> – All but 6 states decreased marijuana possession from a high felony to a low misdemeanor, and the movement towards decriminalization began gaining momentum

<u>1973</u> – Oregon – marijuana possession for personal use becomes a civil infraction, $100 fine

<u>1979</u> – Berkeley, California – enforcing pot prohibitions determined the lowest of all the priorities of the guards, and in the decade preceding the explosion of crack and cocaine this was well advised as those resources were kept proper busy in the years to come

Modern Medical Marijuana

<u>1991</u> – San Francisco, CA – first municipality to pass pro-medical marijuana legislation

<u>1996</u> – California is the first state to legalize medical marijuana, now in 2018 some 29 states and Washington D.C. have medical marijuana statutes in place, with more on the ballot forthcoming

Recreational Marijuana

<u>2012</u> – Washington, and Colorado

<u>2014, Jan.</u> – Colorado – First state to fully legalize and regulate marijuana

<u>2016</u> – Washington D.C., Alaska, California, Colorado, Massachusetts, Maine, Nevada, Oregon, Washington initiate their recreational marijuana programs

State Legalization

In 2016 the see-saw tipped, with over half of the states legalizing medical marijuana. 29 states and Washington D.C. have approved medical marijuana (as per Jan. 2018 data). 9 states and Washington D.C. have approved recreational marijuana

<u>Source</u>: Alicia Wallace, *Where is weed legal? Map of U.S. Marijuana Laws by State,* The Cannabist (Updated January 2018),

https://www.thecannabist.co/2016/10/14/legal-marijuana-laws-by-state-map-united-states/62772/ (last visited Jun. 9, 2018).

Federal Law & The Controlled Substances Act (CSA) of 1970

The CSA classified drugs into 5 schedules, with marijuana at the top of the charts as a schedule 1, the most strictly regulated of all the drugs the man would prefer we not partake in. Schedules are based on: (1) currently accepted medical use of the drug (2) safety of the drug (3) potential for abuse or addiction. Schedule 1s are not allowed for any use, even medical. Marijuana is further classified as a hallucinogen, a lingering misperception from the 1960s.

The penalties for possession outlined by the CSA are harsh. Possession can result in up to 1 year of incarceration, one year more for subsequent possessions. The sale of marijuana is punishable by up to 5 years, and a $250,000 fine. Very few dealers earn anywhere close to that, so such a charge would oftentimes be financially ruinous, and with prosecutors' ability to freeze assets to preclude defense attorneys being paid, even the dealers who could afford it cannot access their cash. Greater than 50 kilos leads to up to life in the cage. Efforts have been undertaken to reschedule marijuana into schedule II, given its state-recognized medical benefits. In 1985, Marinol, a THC derivative, was placed on Schedule II. The DEA argues that this effectively placed a cannabinoid on the Schedule II, and thus reclassifying marijuana is not necessary, yet enforcement measures matching schedule I persist.

The Supreme Court has not determined if the Supremacy Clause preempts State marijuana policy that opposes the CSA. Further, the Supreme Court has not yet decided whether the Feds can compel the states to enforce the CSA. "Anti-commandeering cases" –indicate that the Feds are not allowed to force states to enforce the CSA. Federal power to target marijuana in the states is though to originate in the Commerce Clause and the Necessary and Proper Clause of the Constitution, providing for the "federalization" of crime, yet enforcement measures still do not necessarily pass through over and beyond State powers. Prosecutors must heed the Equal Protection Clause of the 14th Amendment, although systemic racism and socio-economic discrimination in practice largely preclude this.

There are many means, heavily armed and mechanized, through which the CSA is enforced. The DEA MET, Mobile Enforcement Team, is a militarized force that deploys with state and local authorities when violent crime arises linked to marijuana, or is suspected to. The HIDTA, High Intensity Drug Trafficking Areas Program, funds 733 initiatives to promote coordination and intelligence sharing in the 28 regions the program targets, expending vast sums of resources. The OCDETF, Organized Crime Drug Enforcement Task Force Program, runs 11 offices in the nation. Cohesive efforts are coordinated through the Office of National Drug Control Policy, led by the "Drug Czar". The Border Enforcement Security Task Force works with the Department of Homeland Security to protect against drug importation.

The war on drugs keeps the system quite busy, and legalization opposes the profiteering character that has pervaded law enforcement agencies. In 2015 alone the DEA seized some $29.73 million in marijuana cultivator assets. From 1998-2013 there were an average of 5-8,000 annual DEA arrests for marijuana. Marijuana seizures represented 95% of drugs seized in 2013, and of 13,383 federal drug cases filed with U.S. attorneys, 4,942 were for marijuana, 98% of which at least included a drug trafficking offense, exhibiting non-targeting of mere possession.

Advocacy

The year 1972 marked the establishment of NORML, National Organization for the Reform of Marijuana Laws, whose efforts persist into this day. In 1988 then-DEA Chief Administrative Law Judge Francis Young concluded that marijuana was safe for therapeutic purposes and should be reclassified as a Schedule II. The DEA refused to adopt his suggestion. In 2015 the House of Representatives reduced funding to the DEA for cannabis eradication and eliminated funding for the targeting of marijuana activity that complies with state medical legislation, echoing the voice of the people and shifting public opinion in favor of cannabis. Physicians/Doctors are effectively covered by the First Amendment Freedom of Speech in their advocacy of marijuana. They may "recommend" and outline the benefits of marijuana to patients but cannot provide a means to obtain marijuana without violating federal law, entailing the risk "aiding and abetting" as per the CSA.

Local Law

A few key questions on local laws and marijuana answered. (1) Can localities refuse to enforce State marijuana policy? Yes, in fact in Colorado very few localities allow dispensaries, which are largely limited to main cities. (2) Can localities/municipalities legalize or decriminalize in opposition to State and Federal policy? If the state supports it, the municipality may, if illegal in the state, they may not. (3) Are the officers and prosecutors subject to the municipality's or the State's marijuana policies? Yes, depending upon the circumstances and context. Local authorities can be forced to give back confiscated marijuana to those who possessed in line with state law, in Colorado, although in Washington the courts have ruled just the opposite

State Taxation – Medical v. Recreational

In Colorado and Washington, recreational and medical, the taxes on medical marijuana is markedly lower, making it more accessible to patients in need, demonstrating benevolence.

Chapter 2:
Cannabis Case Law

United States v. McIntosh, 833 F.3d 1163 (9th Cir. 2016) – The House of Representative's defunding of the DEA's ability to target state-approved medical weed ops effectively prohibits the federal prosecution of those acting in line with state policy

United States v. White Plume, 2016 WL 1228585 – Uncertainty persists as to whether Native American tribes can grow hemp in Indian Country, with the case seemingly approving it, then disapproving it, with an investment and subsequent divestment through burning the crop being experienced, demonstrating literally the fiery destruction that a vacillating federal government might do to the budding marijuana industry. In 2004 Plume was enjoined from growing, then in July of 2015 filed a motion pursuant to Rule 60(b) seeking to vacate the permanent injunction against growing hemp. Of the reasons allowed under 60(b), Plume was focusing largely upon "…or applying it prospectively is no longer equitable… any other reason that justified relief" and noted that due to the national shift in marijuana policy, the decision should be revisited. "Within a reasonable time" was allowed to extend to over a decade as significant policy changes occurred, making it "reasonable". The injunction was lifted, the legality of the hemp production set aside and not considered. Witness the glory of the Federal Rules of Civil Procedure.

People v. Crouse, No. 12CA2298, 2013 WL 6673708 (Colo. App. Dec. 1, 2013) – upheld the necessity of local police returning confiscated marijuana that was found to be possessed in accordance with state laws, exhibiting the State's preemption of local law.

State v. Ehrensring, 255 Or App 402, 415, 296 P. 3d 1279 (2013) – found in contrast to *People v. Crouse* that for property to be returned it must be legally possessed, and federal law states the herb cannot be legally possessed, and thus cannot be returned.

Mocrieffe v. Holder, 560 S. Ct. 1678 (2013) – U.S. Supreme court ameliorated the deportation requirements for minor marijuana offenses, recognizing proportionality and being reasonable.

Americans for Safe Access v. DEA, 706 F.3d 438 (D.C. Cir. 2013) – Upheld the refusal of the DEA to reschedule marijuana onto Schedule II, recognizing the health benefits thereof. The DEA continues to refuse despite ongoing state legalization of medical marijuana and the recognized benefits thereof.

Gonzales v. Raich, 545 U.S. 1 (2005) – Court held that federal power under the Commerce Clause can extend to purely local conduct, i.e. growing marijuana for personal enjoyment. It was deemed that intrastate cultivation in line with CA law exceeded Congressional authority under the Commerce Clause. At first the Ninth Circuit found the exercise unconstitutional, but a 6-3 decision of the Supreme Court overturned it. Considered the Supremacy Clause and conflict between state v. federal levels. Supreme Court has not discussed, lower courts generally find that federal law does not preempt the field, allowing for the proliferation of cannabis in the States.

Printz v. United States – 521 U.S. 898 (1997) - State law enforcement officials cannot be forced to enforce federal legislation.

New York v. United States, 505 U.S. 144, 188 (1992) – States cannot be compelled to establish a federal regulatory scheme.

Ravin v. State, 537 P.2d 494 (Alaska 1975). Possession decriminalized as the Court determined that the Alaska Constitution preserved an implicit right to privacy, affording persons protection for the possession of small amounts of marijuana kept at home for personal use.

Leary v. United States, 395 U.S. 6 (1969) – Supreme Court struck down the Marihuana Tax Act of 1937 as unconstitutional, and the Narcotic Drugs Import and Export Act of 1954, which created the presumption that mere possession of marijuana meant that the person knew it to have been illegally imported (violating Due Process rights under the 5th Amendment), and thus subject to the mandatory minimum sentence of 5 years as per the Boggs Act. Registration for illicit dealers and users to preclude prosecution was also ruled unconstitutional as a violation of 5th Amendment rights against self-incrimination.

Wickard v. Filburn, 317 U.S. 111 (1942) – extended authority for Congress to regulate intrastate activity on the premise that intrastate activity inadvertently affects national markets, laying the foundation for national drug policy enforcement schemes and their consonant agencies.

United States v. Doremus, 249 U.S. 86 (1919) – Supreme Court upheld the Harrison Narcotics Tax Act of 1914 as a valid exercise of Congress' authority to tax businesses largely selling opium, heroine, and cocaine, despite the fact that some 1% of Americans were at the time addicted to opiates. 5/9 judges felt this way, while 4/9 judges found that the exercise of Congress was unconstitutional and went beyond the power that had been delegated to the federal government, infringing upon spheres thought to be reserved for the police powers of the states.

Chapter III:
Key Cannabis Statutes and Standards

The 8 Points of Priorities for the DOJ – Cannabis Enforcement Standards

1- Prevent the sale of marijuana to minors
2- Preclude weed money from funneling into criminal enterprises
3- Prevent diversion of marijuana products from legal into illegal states
4- Don't allow marijuana to be a mask for harder drug trafficking
5- No violence and shoot-outs
6- Don't drive high, and other public health concerns
7- No growing marijuana plants on public lands
8- No cannabis use or possession on federal property

10th Amendment – "The powers not delegated to the United States by the Constitution, nor prohibited by it to the states, are reserved to the states respectively, or to the people."

Public Law 83-280 PL 280 Tribal Link – passed by Congress, delegating federal law enforcement authority to state jurisdiction, in place in Alaska, California, Minnesota, Nebraska, Oregon, and Wisconsin, thus in legal states, state authorities cannot enforce on tribal lands

Elements of Marijuana…:

Possession – (1) knowledge (2) possession [actual or constructive] (3) quantity of marijuana indicated by the statute.

Selling – (1) knowledge (2) possession (3) the statutory quantity of marijuana (4) intent to sell. Often the government will use Federal Rules of Evidence 402 and 403 to exclude proof that the marijuana was for personal use, elevating from possession to sale to gain court advantage.

Paraphernalia – (1) knowledge (2) possession of items commonly used for marijuana consumption and intending such use.

Federal Issues with Marijuana

41 C.F.R. § 102-74.400 – marijuana is prohibited on all federal properties

Executive Order 12564 (1986) – federal employees cannot smoke weed on or off the job

41 U.S.C. § 8101-8106- federal contractors and grant recipients must maintain drug-free workplaces or lose their funding

Rohrbacher-Farr Amendment - precludes the DOJ from acting against state medical marijuana legislation

The Memos on Marijuana

Ogden Memorandum – 2009 - if states meet the eight enforcement standards, non-targeting or intervention policy

Cole Memorandum I and II 2013&14– first one was fear, many dispensaries busted, while the second relaxes and pull back, again noting the 8 standards

Banking Memorandum – 2014 - Non-enforcement against banks working w/ companies in compliance with the 8 standards, excepting money laundering issues

Marijuana Issues in Indian Country – 2014 – meet the 8 standards, and tribes left to establish and play an equal role in marijuana policy on Tribal reservations

War on Drugs Statutes

18 U.S.C. §§ 922(g)(3), 929(a)(2); 27 C.F.R. § 478.11 (106) – ATF Form 4473 – Question 11e – does an applicant exercising their Founding Father given right to bear arms is asked if they are "an unlawful user of, or addicted to, marijuana", with a false answer bearing a 5 year maximum period in the concrete jungle. What of states in which marijuana is legal, eh?

21 U.S.C. § 844 – Possession - first possession a misdemeanor, up to 1 year and a minimum fine of $1,000. Second offense 15 days to 2 years, up to $2,500. Third of subsequent, 90 days to 3 years, minimum fine of $5,000.

21 U.S.C. § 841 – Trafficking – less than 50kg, or 10kg of hashish, or 1kg of oil, or 1-49 plants, up to 5 years and max fine of $250,000. 50-99kg, 50-99 plants, up to 20 years and $1 mil. 100-999kg or 100-999 plants, 40 years and $5 mil. 1,000 or more kg or plants, minimum 10 years maximum life, $10 mil fine.

*trafficking of over 5g to minors (21+) or w/i 1,000ft of a school, university, public housing project, youth center, video arcade, public swimming pool, or playground, doubles the punishment outlined above

21 U.S.C. § 863 – paraphernalia – felony, up to 3 years

21 U.S.C. § 853, 881 – Forfeiture – drugs and money in transaction, and real and personal property substantially connected to the illegal transaction – forfeits to U.S.

21 U.S.C. § 853 – Seizures – criminal forfeiture, only a preponderance of evidence standard, not beyond a reasonable doubt like the rest of the criminal proceeding

21 U.S.C. §881 – civil asset forfeiture – "preponderance of the evidence" to seize property linked to drug crimes, burden of proof on government

USSG – § 2D1.1 - United States Sentencing Guidelines - 1 plant equals 100 grams, or the actual weight thereof if greater than 100 grams

*Collateral consequences – civil sanctions – right to vote, hold office, serve on a jury, in the military, to receive federal benefits. Impact on employment, professional licensing, and even immigration status.

Immigration Issues and Marijuana

Between 2007-2012 33,337 people were deported for marijuana possession convictions, and 18,151 deported for marijuana sale convictions, how this is shifting and evolving in the era of legalization will provide immigration attorneys will a dynamic field of practice.

8 U.S.C. § 1227(a)(2)(B)(i) – INS exception established to deportation for a single offense involving possession of marijuana in a weight less than 30

grams, just under an ounce, for personal use. But does the 1g weight of the bag count? An ounce weighs 28.5g, so even with the 1g of the bag, there is a .5g differential. Possession of an ounce and a bag, non-deportable now.

Chapter IV:
"Native Marijuana"

See below for the abstract to my scholarly legal article, "Native Marijuana: American Indian Sovereignty v. Federal Drug Policy", currently under review at the American Indian Law Journal, followed by an original interview I conducted from therein with the Tribal Leader of a Native Tribe of North America, Mrs. Cheryl Andrews-Maltais of the Wampanoag Tribe of Gay Head (Aquinnah), situated on the red cliffs at Martha's Vineyard in the Cape of Massachusetts.

Abstract:

As the Native Tribes of North America increasingly become involved in the marijuana industry, the overlapping sphere of sovereignty between American Indian Tribes and the Federal Government of the United States is increasingly contentious. Through the issuance of the "Policy Statement Regarding Marijuana Issues in Indian Country" the United States Department of Justice effectively announced a policy of self-governance on behalf of the Native Tribes of North America, yet enforcement efforts continue to expand, bringing rise to questionable violations of sovereign American Indian rights. The Constitutional allowances held by particular Tribes in terms of peyote are explored, reinforcing the unique sovereign position of federally-recognized American Indian tribes. The supportive efforts of the Menominee Indian Tribe of Wisconsin and the Squaxin Island Tribe of Washington are presented to show how Tribes are advocating on behalf of the growth of the marijuana industry. Comparatively, the arduous opposition engaged in on behalf of the Yakama Nation of Washington in concert with the DEA and Bureau of Indian Affairs, and the efforts of the Pit River Tribe of California, are considered to exhibit active American Indian opposition to the growth of the marijuana industry on Tribal lands. To add to the discussion, an original interview with Chairwoman of the Wampanoag Tribe of Gay Head (Aquinnah), Mrs. Cheryl Andrews-Maltais, advances the perspective of a Native Tribal Leader in terms of the potential of marijuana industrialization for American Indian Tribes, and the intersection between Federal and American Indian sovereignty that it represents. As is clearly demonstrated, the marijuana industry holds vast economic potential for the Native Tribes of North America, insofar as the legal maze between American Indian and Federal sovereignty is effectively navigated, and ultimately, American Indian sovereignty is respected.

Interview with Tribal Chairwoman Mrs. Cheryl Andrews-Maltais of the Wampanoag Tribe at Gay Head (Aquinnah)

To provide an intimate and in-depth perspective on the matter the Chairwoman of the Wampanoag Tribe of Gay Head (Aquinnah) Cheryl Andrews kindly accepted a request to engage in an interview to contribute to the discourse. The issues of American Indian sovereignty and the impact this has upon the economic potential of marijuana, and the enforcement measures surrounding such endeavors, are provided further insight. Chairwoman Andrews-Maltais advocates for the capacity of the sovereign Tribes of Indian Country to exercise their power, within the confines of pre-existing agreements and parameters, stating:

> I fully believe, endorse and fight for Tribal Sovereignty and Tribes' rights to do what we feel is in the best interests of

our Tribal Communities. The issue is the conflict between state and federal law and as you know, the federal law is supreme. In my opinion, a Tribe could cultivate, harvest and sell anything that is legal in a state on Tribally owned land; but at the moment that land ownership needs to be on regular fee simple land or any land ownership type that has no federal nexus.[1]

The ownership status of the land is impactful upon the capacity of the Tribe to exercise its sovereignty due to the state-federal interplay, a key issue in marijuana law that had bled over into American Indian law. Of the interplay between American Indian sovereignty, and the balance of power between the state and federal government, Chairwoman Andrews-Maltais noted:

> In conducting activities that are lawful within a jurisdiction to which a Tribe agrees, then their Sovereign immunity should protect them from any litigation unless the Tribe waives that immunity. However, if a Tribe wishes to conduct an activity that's against federal law, and the land is held in trust or restricted fee by the United States, then until or unless the federal government decriminalizes the activity, it remains illegal and should not be conducted on those federally held lands.[2]

The recognition of the division of power has been noted by the tribes explored above, with the threat of federal enforcement action over activities legal in the state extending to Indian Country. The overall

---

[1] Interview with Cheryl Andrews-Maltais, Chairwoman, The Wampanoag Tribe of Gay Head (Aquinnah) (Jan. 22, 2018).
[2] Ibid.

enforcement policy surrounding marijuana endorsed by the federal government is well-heeded by Chairwoman Andrews-Maltais, recognizing that:

> The work-around for this during the Obama administration was that since the administrative branch can't make or change laws, they can establish policies and priorities; committing to or not to act in certain situations in certain circumstances as an agency "policy" regarding a specific or challenging issue. For example, AG Holder (and Rice) had a policy that, as a matter of prioritization of limited funds and resources, they would not investigate or prosecute this activity on Tribal lands when conducted by a Tribal governments' duly authorized entity.[3]

A lack of enforcement measures would seemingly preclude Tribes' marijuana industries from federal enforcement, however, as exhibited above concerning the Pit River Tribe, federal power has been extended over sovereign American Indian territory to an extent opposed by the Tribes. The importance of clarity provides the foundation for growth, and the determination of real policy, as explained by Chairwoman Andrews-Maltais:

> This "neutral" DOJ position appeared to open the door to the potential economic development benefits this endeavor could yield. That opened door also led several Tribes to heavily invest in research and development, patent development and approvals, as well as internal legal and regulatory structures, codes and ordinances. This exercise

---

[3] Interview with Cheryl Andrews-Maltais, Chairwoman, The Wampanoag Tribe of Gay Head (Aquinnah) (Jan. 22, 2018).

of Tribal governance provided two fundamental building blocks to be prepared for an ultimate challenge to the DOJ policy.

One aspect was to establish an exclusively Tribal legal and regulatory structure for the endeavor; demonstrating Tribes' ability to establish and maintain a high level of competency, control and adjudication under its sole jurisdiction. These structures were also established to set the stage for the anticipated legal challenges that would eventually come, due to the federal/state legal conflict.[4]

To support the capacity of the tribes to regulate their marijuana industries, the ability to regulate and enforce the industry internally is necessary. In the Yakama nation, errant non-Tribal marijuana criminals are utilizing tribal land to illegally cultivate marijuana, drawing the attention of the Bureau of Indian Affairs alongside the DEA.[5] Chairwoman Andrews-Maltais has made a similar observation, finding that:

> Demonstrating Tribal regulatory and enforcement capabilities over such an endeavor would prove to fortify the Tribes' position; that provided the endeavor is not a menace to public health or safety (as states have determined), then Congress can take individual or universal action to assure Tribes will be free from prosecution to

---

[4] Interview with Cheryl Andrews-Maltais, Chairwoman, The Wampanoag Tribe of Gay Head (Aquinnah) (Jan. 22, 2018).
[5] Amy Harris, *Marijuana growers find cover on tribal lands,* SEATTLE TIMES (Aug. 23, 2011), https://www.seattletimes.com/seattle-news/marijuana-growers-find-cover-on-tribal-lands/.

enjoy the same sovereign governmental benefits as the states do.[6]

Effectively establishing marijuana industries, whether recreational or medicinal, requires structure in terms of both policy and business. To cultivate the economic benefits of marijuana, it is essential that a forward-thinking perspective be adopted, while still considering the context of the past and present. As conclusively stated by Chairwoman Andrews-Maltais:

> Like in most places, Indian Country is predominantly in favor of medicinal use. However, it is very much split regarding recreational use, particularly due to the alcohol and drug dependency and addiction in Indian Country. And we are acutely all too aware that all money isn't good money, and if the potential detriments outweighs the potential benefits to your individual Tribal Community, then it's best to take the necessary time to fully and carefully weigh the impacts on the futures of your People.[7]

Within the context of states, or the sovereign entities that comprise the various nations of the Tribes of the United States of America, marijuana presents an epically significant tax advantage insofar as it is effectively structured and legalized. The state of Colorado generates substantial capital in tax revenues annually, and has begun to reinvest this capital into essential social programs such as education, and drug addiction services. School systems and ailing members of society are benefitting from the sizeable and growing revenues realized through

---

[6] Interview with Cheryl Andrews-Maltais, Chairwoman, The Wampanoag Tribe of Gay Head (Aquinnah) (Jan. 22, 2018).
[7] Interview with Cheryl Andrews-Maltais, Chairwoman, The Wampanoag Tribe of Gay Head (Aquinnah) (Jan. 22, 2018).

marijuana.[8] The refusal of the federal government to legalize, and ideally nationalize, the marijuana industry is denying the nation countless billions of dollars in related tax revenues, the medical benefits of the substance notwithstanding. The continued imbalanced exercise of marijuana enforcement policy is an ongoing injustice experienced by the sovereign American Indian nations.

Conclusory Comments

Marijuana in the United States holds immense potential for our economy and our people. The effective capitalization of this opportunity depends upon the successful navigation of the cannabis industry through the labyrinthine interplay between state and federal law currently surrounding the issue. Marijuana, all stigmas removed, could and should be perceived in a manner no different than tobacco or alcohol, a legal, taxable substance that of-age Americans are capable of exercising their right to life, liberty, and the pursuit of happiness to enjoy.

---

[8] Jennifer Calfas, *How Colorado's Booming Marijuana Industry is Helping Fight Homelessness and Drug Addiction,* TIME (Jun. 1, 2017), http://time.com/money/4801768/colorado-marijuana-industry-tax-revenue/.

Up next will be my "Cannabis Law Case Book: Clearing the Smoke", tentatively titled. Until then, stay lifted and stay legal.

Cheers,

-MJW

About the author:

American writer, law student, marijuana advocate, and future cannabis attorney. Resident of the South Coast in Massachusetts, driver of e34 BMWs, practitioner of yoga and wing chun kung fu, and proud owner of two of the cutest dogs in the nation. Michael has an eclectic professional past including international comic-book publishing in Boston, screenwriting and journalism in SoCal, online content writing, and live-event mixology craft services, retail signature cocktail simple syrup branding/sales, and event curation in Austin. At the moment Michael is pursuing a juris doctorate at the University of Massachusetts School of Law to hone the skills necessary to take up a position at the vanguard of the national cannabis industry, facilitating its positive social impact through practicing as a marijuana lawyer and advocate.

© 2018 Michael John Westerman

www.ingramcontent.com/pod-product-compliance
Lightning Source LLC
Chambersburg PA
CBHW031517210526
45464CB00007B/2948